To:

From:

Wisdom from

FINDING
YOUR OWN
NORTH
STAR

claiming the life you
were meant to live

M A R T H A   B E C K

Peter Pauper Press, Inc.
White Plains, New York

The text in this book is excerpted from
Finding Your Own North Star
Claiming the Life You Were Meant to Live
by Martha Beck, originally published by
Crown Publishers in 2001.
Copyright © 2001 by Martha Beck
All rights reserved

Designed by Taryn R. Sefecka

Published in 2005 by arrangement with
Three Rivers Press, a division of Random House, Inc.
Peter Pauper Press, Inc.
202 Mamaroneck Avenue
White Plains, NY 10601
All rights reserved
ISBN 1-59359-979-X
Printed in China
7 6 5 4 3 2 1

Wisdom from

FINDING YOUR OWN

NORTH

STAR

claiming the life you
were meant to live

CONTENTS

INTRODUCTION

Right in the middle of my life, I realized that I wasn't where I wanted to be. It was like I'd wandered off the right path into a very, very bad neighborhood. I don't even want to remember how scary that space was—makes me feel like I'm gonna die or something. I'm only telling you about it because a lot of good came of it in the long run. So anyway,

I don't even know how I ended up so far off course. I felt like I'd been sleepwalking. —DAN, AGE 41

THIS STORY could have come from any one of the hundreds of people I've met in my office, classes, and seminars, but it didn't. As a matter of fact, "Dan" is short for Dante, as in Dante Alighieri. The paragraph above is my own exceedingly loose rendition of the first twelve lines of *The Divine Comedy,* written in 1307. Sometimes I tell clients about it, because it helps them believe they aren't the first people who've ever snapped awake at midlife, only to find themselves dazed, unhappy, and way off course. It's been happening at least since the Middle Ages, and not only to the middle-aged.

There are as many paths as there are people, and the only one I can chart is my own. I have no idea, for example, where your true path may lie. But you do.

I believe that a knowledge of that perfect life sits inside you just as the North Star sits in its unalterable spot.

You may think you're utterly lost, that you're going to die a bewildered death in the Dark Wood of Error. But brush away the leaves, wait for the clouds to clear, and you'll see your destiny shining as brightly as ever: the fixed point in the constantly changing constellations of your life.

THE
DISCONNECTED SELF

I BASE ALL MY COUNSELING on the premise that each of us has these two sides: the essential self and the social self. The essential self contains several sophisticated compasses that continuously point toward your North Star. The social self is the set of skills that actually carry you toward this goal.

This system functions beautifully

as long as the social and essential selves are communicating freely with each other and working in perfect synchrony. However, not many people are lucky enough to experience such inner harmony. ... The vast majority of us put other people in charge of charting our course through life. Naturally, they end up sending us off course.

Your essential self formed before you were born, and it will remain until you've shuffled off your mortal coil. It's the basic you, stripped of options and special features. It is "essential" in two ways: first, it is the essence of your personality, and second, you absolutely need it to find your North Star.

The social self, on the other hand, is the part of you that developed in response to pressures from the people around you, including everyone from your family to your first love to the pope.

Between birth and this moment, your social self has picked up a huge variety of skills. It learned to talk, read, dress, dance, drive, juggle, merge, acquire, cook, yodel, wait in line, share bananas, restrain the urge to bite—anything that won social approval.

YOUR TWO SELVES:
BASIS OF OPERATIONS

Behaviors of the Social Self Are:	Behaviors of the Essential Self Are:
• Avoidance-based	• Attraction-based
• Conforming	• Unique
• Imitative	• Inventive
• Predictable	• Surprising
• Planned	• Spontaneous
• Hardworking	• Playful

RECONNECTING: HOW YOUR ESSENTIAL SELF SAYS "NO"

JAMES SAID HE WAS RUINING his life by "flaking out" every time he got his career on track and straightened out his relationship with his parents. His pattern was to start showing up late—or worse, forgetting to show up at all—for office meetings or social events with his family. Dorrie's problem was that her mind "froze" whenever she had to give presentations, an important part of her job. Kurt had a little anger-management problem: He'd ruined any number of personal and professional relationships by starting shouting matches over trivial issues.

As these people examined their lives, they all found that their "self-sabotage" was actually in harmony with their essential desires.

When you leave your true path and start heading away from your

North Star, your essential self will use any or all of its skills and tools to stop you. If your social self won't pay attention to mild warnings, the essential self has to get more and more dramatic. Fortunately, you can avoid such unpleasant situations if you learn just one "word" in your essential self's non-verbal lexicon: NO.

Teaching your social self to pay attention when your essential self says "no" is the most basic way to reconnect the two sides of your personality.

That feeling of choked hostility, or numb depression, or nauseated helplessness is a sure sign you're steering away from your North Star, toward a life you were *not* meant to live. *When you feel it, you must change course.* You must say to people around you what your essential self is saying inside: "Nope. Not going there. Not doing that. Sorry, but the answer is no."

GETTING TO YES

THE MECHANISMS your essential self uses to shut down or sabotage your social self whenever you're headed away from your North Star are the same ones it uses to say *"Yes!"*

Nothing is too large or too small to affect your progress toward your North Star. By noticing ... good moods and pursuing the activities that produce them, you reconnect yourself with the navigational instruments that lead to your true path.

When I ask people to remember the happy times in their lives, they often get downright confrontational. "Are you telling me to quit my job?" they'll demand, or "Are you telling me I'm in the wrong relationship?" I haven't told them anything of the kind. ... But as soon as these people reconnect with genuinely positive feelings, their essential selves begin to suggest major life remodeling. This can be mighty frightening. If it happens to you, please don't get your knickers in a knot.

You don't have to do one single thing right now except reconnect your social and essential selves.

JUST BECAUSE YOU'RE PARANOID DOESN'T MEAN EVERYBODY ISN'T OUT TO GET YOU

DON'T LOOK NOW, but a lot of very powerful people are trying to stop you from reaching your North Star. Who are they? *Everybody,* that's who. The social self isn't opposed to your reaching your North Star, per se; it just won't allow you to proceed toward it until you get Everybody's permission.

... I'd bet my purple socks that your Everybody is not really representative of the human species. I'd also bet that you are creating many of the reactions you expect to see in the people around you. If so, then looking closely at your Everybody (tearing it into little bits, if necessary) is the first step toward breaking destructive patterns and finding support and encouragement in your quest for your own North Star.

GETTING
EVERYBODY ON
YOUR SIDE

IF YOU CAN CONVINCE [the social self] that Everybody approves of your true path—and … the social self needs only three or four opinions to draw this conclusion—it will automatically begin to disassemble the barriers that keep you from your own North Star.

The important thing is to tell yourself a life story in which you, the hero, are primarily a problem solver rather than a helpless victim.

Spend as much time as possible with people who support your true self. Spend as little time as possible with those who don't.

Make a regular practice of this and you'll eventually end up finding the best of all Everybodies: your very own tribe.

Despite our individualistic culture's pretense that we can all build our dreams by our little lonesomes, the truth is that we must have social support to do something as audacious as finding our own North Stars. Before you head out on your journey, and all along the way, take the time to get and keep Everybody on your side. You need it, and you deserve it. Everybody thinks so.

SOUL SHRAPNEL: REPAIRING YOUR EMOTIONAL COMPASS

Every neurosis is a substitute for legitimate suffering.

—CARL JUNG

MOST OF MY CLIENTS expect that as soon as they get in touch with their essential selves, they'll discover a passion, talent, or ambition that will propel them instantly to wealth and glory. In some cases, that's exactly what happens. More often, however, the first thing the essential self manages to communicate is pain. And the first thing it cries out for is surgery.

Your emotions are incredibly powerful, precise navigational tools, custom-made to help you find and reach your own North Star. However, many of us have encountered circumstances that damaged our emotional compasses.

Even if you achieve things that seem outwardly fabulous, an unhealed emotional injury will make you experience them as empty and unappealing. By contrast, recovering your emotional health will suffuse even small successes with joy, long before you achieve anything obviously spectacular.

Once it's been diagnosed, fixing the damage from emotional wounds is surprisingly simple. I said simple, not easy. The steps are pretty straightforward, but they're guaranteed to scare you, and they may be briefly but intensely painful.

1) First, you have to locate any damaging alien objects that may be lodged in your psyche. This is done by searching your memory for the events that caused your emotional injury.

2) To clean out your wounds, you must identify at least one person who can hear your story with compassion and empathy. The ultimate goal of this step is to learn self-love.

3) Whether you're talking to yourself or a confidant... give this person a full account of the events that hurt you. Include your emotional reactions to the events.

4) The equivalent of stitching up the cleaned wound happens when you get a compassionate response from your listener, allow yourself to accept that love, and begin to feel it toward yourself.

5) Even after the first four steps have been completed, you may need to rest a bit while you finish healing.

Healing your emotional wounds means shattering the soft-focus lens of denial that pretties up ugly truths of family history and personal experience. It also means taking responsibility for your own misdeeds, whatever they may be.

From the first time you tell your truths and are truly understood, you'll begin to experience surges of unprecedented happiness.

As a kind of by-product, you may wake up one morning to discover that you have forgiven the people who hurt you.

Once it's whole, your emotional self won't let you rest until you're moving straight toward your North Star.

READING
YOUR EMOTIONAL
COMPASS

OFTEN, MY CLIENTS have no idea what emotions they're feeling. Their social selves exist in a state of bland pleasantness, or perhaps glum depression, that hides the raw emotional experience of the essential self. To get a general heading from your emotional compass, you might want to use what I call the Four Magic Questions. As you read through the explanations below, try answering each question for yourself.

Magic Question No. 1:

What Am I Feeling?

If you're feeling a confusing welter of emotions, try categorizing the sensation into one of four major areas: sad, mad, glad, or scared. Doing so seems to prime the pump, allowing people to get more specific, subtle emotional information. Once you get used to doing this, you may get so good at expressing every nuance of feeling that you start spouting extemporaneous poetry.

Magic Question No. 2:

Why Am I Feeling This Way?

The only way out of a "complicated" emotional situation is to figure out which feelings are coming directly from your core and which are being imposed on you by social fears and obligations. The result may unnerve you by presenting you with a choice to either follow your own instincts or obey frustrating social imperatives, but it won't be all that complicated.

Magic Question No. 3:

What Will It Take to Make Me Happy?

You're the only person who can figure out exactly what would make you happy. It's your job to define and articulate your needs. Even if others were willing to do it, the fact is that *they can't*. If your needs are being frustrated by another person's behavior, it's especially important to ask "Why?" enough times to reach the root of your feelings, where they can be expressed in terms of your needs, not other people's behavior.

Magic Question No. 4:

What's the Most Effective Way to Get What I Want?

So far … this book has focused on silencing your social self long enough to hear the directives of your essential self. However, once you've gone inward to pinpoint exactly what you want, your social self should be invited back to help you complete your journey. Magic Question No. 4 is the point at which this happens.

Figuring out the most effective way of getting what you want often takes the form of a dialogue between your essential and social selves. The essential self will come up with wild, out-of-the-box, often unworkable ideas. The social self's solutions often lack pizzazz, but they tend to work.

CHARTING
YOUR COURSE

EMOTIONAL ENERGY always creates change. If that energy is handled well, the change will move you closer to the life you want. However, most of us don't get much instruction about using our emotional power effectively. In the grip of passion, we're about as effective as five-year-olds trying to operate a nuclear submarine.

Emotion is a glorious force that will push you toward your North Star with breathtaking speed and efficiency. When your social self uses its tremendous powers of restraint and guidance to shape behaviors based on your real desires, instead of in opposition to them, you will be astonished by your own power.

IF YOUR EMOTIONAL
COMPASS READS "FEAR"

FEAR TELLS YOU that something in your immediate vicinity is threatening your progress toward happiness. To move forward, you must make some move that will cause your fear to dissipate as soon as possible.

Fear is a particularly common stand-in for other emotions. Real fear is easy to distinguish from the phony variety, because it has a clear source and motivates clear action. Fake fear is a blanket anxiety or worry that doesn't mobilize; on the contrary, it paralyzes.

If something is scaring you, *learn everything about it that you possibly can.*

If fear and desire give the same instructions, run away. If fear and desire give opposite instructions, feel your fear and stand your ground.

In other words, you should run from anything that scares you and holds absolutely no appeal for your essential self. If the thought of attending medical school makes you queasy with dread and you've never for one second wanted to be a doctor, *stay away from medical school.*

On the other hand, there will be many instances when fear and desire point in opposite directions. You want something, but you're scared to go for it. This kind of fear—the fear that accompanies desire—is something you must face, not flee, to reach your own North Star.

EXERCISE

1) Complete this sentence:
If I only had the guts, I would …

....

....

2) Whatever you just wrote down,
do it. Right now.

If you begin to face your fears, something bittersweet is going to happen
to you: … you'll realize that fear is
the raw material from which courage
is manufactured. Without it, we
wouldn't even know what it means to
be brave.

IF YOUR EMOTIONAL
COMPASS READS "GRIEF"

PEOPLE WHO FOLLOW grief through its whole course emerge stronger and healthier, more able to cope with the inevitable losses that affect every human life.

People who don't honor their losses don't grieve. They may lose all joy in living, but they don't actively mourn, and this means that they don't heal.

EXERCISE

Is there any sadness you carry that has not been honored, either by you or by the people around you? What is it?

Now give yourself permission to grieve this loss, no matter now "inappropriate" or silly it might seem. Processing genuine grief is never inappropriate. It's the only way to your North Star.

Our deepest grief...is reserved for things that have no acceptable substitutes: loved ones, relationships, health, hopes, dreams. If you've suffered this kind of a loss, the road to your North Star lies through grieving. There's nothing to do but mourn, and the pain will disappear a lot faster if you lean into it. Normal grieving follows its own course. You can no more force it to hurry up than you can force a broken bone to knit *right now*. To get into—or, more accurately, through—your grief, you have to make a safe place for mourning. At a bare minimum, you need privacy and quiet. Ideally, you'll have a warm, comfortable place where you can lie down and wrap yourself in a blanket or two.

You should definitely do things that gladden your heart during a period of mourning, but you'll find that your heart has odd preferences at such a time. Whatever works best for you, add it to your day. It's the best way to get to the time when you really will feel like dancing.

No moment, however sweet, can last. On the other hand, neither will pain or sorrow—not if you allow them to flow freely. Losing the illusion of permanence means that you will accept your losses. People who don't resist grief, who let it flow through them, come out more resilient on the other side. Ironically, it is those who have accepted the most terrible grief who are capable of the greatest joy.

IF YOUR EMOTIONAL COMPASS READS "ANGER"

ANGER... IS THE PSYCHOLOGICAL equivalent of the immune system. It is triggered whenever we perceive injustice, giving us strength and energy to change the status quo. Anger is like fire in the soul. Repressed, it destroys from the inside, by slow burn or explosion. Misdirected, it can blaze a path of destruction through your life and the lives of others. Cared for and properly used, it can warm you, light your path, fuel your progress, and keep hostile interlopers at bay.

When you're genuinely angry, it means one of two things: either something that your essential self needs is absent, or something your essential self can't tolerate is present. To make the anger go away, you have to change this situation.

No matter how frightening or irrational your anger may seem, acknowledging that you are angry is the first step toward a peaceful and cooperative connection with the world around you.

You can change yourself or you can change the situation that's making you angry. A third option—carrying all that anger around with you, not changing anything—is a recipe for disaster.

Sometimes, the reason for your anger will be someone else. . . . In this case, you may have to "fight" to change the situation. Here are some rules for doing that responsibly and effectively.

Step 1:
Burn off "hot" anger before the confrontation.

- Use the energy of rage constructively, not destructively.

Step 2:
Using "cool" anger for energy, confront the person who's responsible for your anger. Tell him or her exactly what's bothering you, and why.

- Use examples to support all generalities.

- Speak only in terms of your own firsthand experience.

- Don't moralize; just express your feelings.

Step 3:
Tell the other person exactly what you'd like him or her to do.

Step 4:
Spell out what you'll do if nothing changes, and follow through.

If you follow the steps I've just described, your anger will push you toward your own North Star like rocket fuel. It will also rob you of the illusion that you are helpless to change your situation.

Giving up your illusion of helplessness leaves you staring at the raw truth: that no one else is totally responsible for your failures, and no one else can push you into the success you deserve.

IF YOUR EMOTIONAL COMPASS READS "JOY"

THERE ARE TWO RULES for using joy to chart a course for your own North Star.

Rule 1:
If it brings you joy, do it.

Rule 2:
No, really. If it brings you joy, do it.

In fact, if the only thing you ever did was fill your life with the people, things, and activities that bring you genuine joy, you'd find your own North Star almost immediately.

To chart your course in life by the compass of joy, you must first understand how genuine, core-deep happiness looks, feels, sounds, smells, and tastes.

REAL JOY

THIS KIND OF JOY, the kind that runs deep and broad, requires facing and mastering all the painful experiences we've discussed in the previous sections. It means making yourself stand and face the things you fear long before you've had a chance to develop courage; allowing grief to wash over you when you really think you'll drown in it; channeling rage into compassionate action when you long to commit mayhem. To chart your course by joy, you need a strong moral center and some serious guts.

FAKE JOY

THE BIGGEST DANGER you face when dealing with happiness is mistaking joy substitutes for the real thing. Phony joy takes you to a place of ecstasy, then drops you off the edge of a cliff. This is true not only of chemical euphoria but of any mood-altering substance or activity.

MAXIMIZING YOUR LIFE'S JOY CONTENT

PUTTING JOYFUL ACTIVITIES into every nook and cranny of your day is a great way to start toward your North Star. When you start doing what you love, you're likely to do it very well, with zest, skill, and infectious delight.

The confidence that your capacity to experience joy is internal and indestructible grows as you let go of joyful experiences and find that they are replaced by others even more wonderful.

The truth is that people will love you much more honestly and easily if you give up suffering and fill your life with joy.

A MAP OF CHANGE

PEOPLE WHO'VE BEEN LIVING the
right life all along simply pick up the
pace and intensity when they locate
their North Stars. It's usually a lot of
fun. But for a person who's stuck in
the wrong life, setting out on a North
Star quest has all the combined attrac-
tions of suicide and childbirth. To
complete it, you'll have to kill off the
old You and give birth to a different

You, someone nobody has ever seen before.

Though no one can tell you where your life changes will take you, *the process of life change itself follows a predictable course.* Every major transformation will take you through a similar sequence of events.

Life transformation follows a cyclical course, one you've already negotiated several times.

THE CHANGE CYCLE

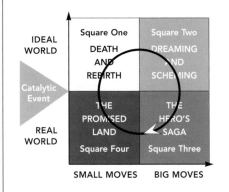

IDEAL WORLD

Catalytic Event

REAL WORLD

Square One
DEATH AND REBIRTH

Square Two
DREAMING AND SCHEMING

THE PROMISED LAND
Square Four

THE HERO'S SAGA
Square Three

SMALL MOVES   BIG MOVES

IN CHEMISTRY, something that starts a reaction is called a "catalyst." In the change cycle, it means any event that pitches you into a major life transition. The change is so big, in fact, that it ends up redefining the way you see yourself. Catalytic changes literally *transform your identity* in your own eyes, and usually the eyes of others, so that you are identified by a new label.

Catalytic events fall into three types: shock, opportunity, and transition. They make it necessary for you to chart a new course through life, and they free you to find your essential self, consult your internal compasses, and choose to go in the direction of joy and fulfillment.

A shock is a sudden change that comes from outside you. An opportunity *always* looks like a lucky break. Transition events develop much more slowly than shocks or opportunities, and they come from inside you, rather than from the environment.

Whatever type of change catalyst you experience, it throws you into the first phase of change. I call this phase Square One, because clients who launch themselves into a new life often tell me they feel that they've gone "back to square one."

SQUARE ONE:
DEATH AND REBIRTH

*I am crossing the bridges
of sorrow,
Empty with yearning and
full of tomorrow.*

—OCTOBER PROJECT

THE CHANGE CYCLE doesn't begin when we experience the minor course corrections of life, only when something forces us to *let go of our identities.* This is a very real and profound form of annihilation.

Each of us has infinite roles and identities. But we typically think of just a few, maybe only one, when we say, "This is what I am." This "primary identity" shapes our place in the world, dictates many of our actions, helps us feel that our lives are grounded and meaningful. . . . *It could all go away, any time.*

Even when the change is what we want, entering Square One means enduring loss after loss after loss. The "death" component of Square One, that initial period when you first come to terms with the fact that your old identity is lost, can only be managed by grieving.

The beginning of Square One, the departure from your old life, will feel slightly different depending on whether the "catalytic event" that shoved you out of your old identity was a shock, an opportunity, or a transition.

You may not be even remotely responsible for causing the shocks in your own life, so you don't have many clues about when they'll arrive or what form they might take.... One thing you must remember after a shock is that you should *make no big decisions until the dust has settled.*

In some ways, opportunity catalysts can be even more terrifying than shocks. After all, if fate deals you a totally unforeseen blow, all anyone will expect you to do is survive and cope. A huge opportunity, on the other hand, *always* means a huge

challenge. ... To be a true change catalyst, an opportunity has to stretch
you way beyond your limits. And that
means *fear.*

Transition events are even more
likely to cause social disruption—and
intense self-doubt—than opportunities. When you change your whole
life because of inner yearning, frustra-
tion, or excitement, there's no exter-
nal force or prize to help other people
accept your behavior.

Whatever you do to cope as you
struggle to accept your own "death,"
stay in touch with the real you.

Refuse to abandon your essential self, the way a great captain refuses to abandon his ship.

THE THRESHOLD

SINCE YOU'VE LOST your old identity but haven't really embraced a new one, you're temporarily a kind of nobody.

When your whole life is changing, it's normal to have lots of ideas about what you might do. Now is the time to *play* with these ideas, not to lock yourself into ironclad plans.

Wait until an idea has felt right for a number of days or weeks before you commit to making it a part of your new life.

Part of making small moves is keeping your attention focused on the here and now. Your life has changed. *You* have changed. Moving forward may be scary, humiliating, and painful, but going back is impossible.

Remember and repeat the
SQUARE ONE MANTRA:

I don't know what the hell is going on, and that's okay.

Learning about a new situation or task requires admitting—sometimes only to yourself, but often to others as well—that you are as rank a beginner as any five-year-old. If you acknowledge your ignorance to *everyone* who can help you, you'll not only get a grip on the situation much faster but also earn these people's friendship and respect.

On the threshold, your essential self has more freedom than at any other time or place.

Consider just letting yourself relax into the "not-thinking" and "not-doing" Taoist masters worked so hard to achieve. Sit with the nothingness until your fear fades. Watch what—and who—emerges.

REBIRTH

AS YOU WANDER around the nothingness of the threshold, follow your internal compasses *no matter where they take you.* Just keep doing what feels most joyful, and eventually, in ways you never imagined, you'll come upon your own North Star.

As the world spins crazily around you, pay attention to what I call the "three N's": noticing what you love, narrowing your focus, and, finally, naming the thing you most desire, the identity that fits as though it's custom-tailored.

When you're doing what you're meant to do, you benefit the world in a unique and irreplaceable way. This brings money, friendship, true love, inner peace, and everything else worth having; it sounds facile, but it's really true.

SQUARE TWO:
DREAMING AND
SCHEMING

*We are such stuff
as dreams are made on.*

—WILL S.

HOPE—REAL, SPONTANEOUS HOPE, with its accompanying excitement and delight—is the key signal that you're moving out of Square One and into Square Two of the change cycle.

No two people experience exactly the same complex of symptoms, and only the spontaneous dreaming is a true indicator. However, you'll probably notice some of these as you arrive at Square Two:

1) You laugh more easily and more often.

2) You want to do things you've never done.

3) Your creativity returns.

4) You change your clothes.

5) You change your hair.

6) You remodel, redecorate, or renovate your living space.

As you begin to notice symptoms of Square Two, you'll also see your attention naturally shifting from small, adaptive moves to longer-term plans.

You have to prepare for the major life changes of Square Three by dreaming, and dreaming big. This means valuing and nourishing every dream that pops into your head during Square Two—even if they seem like far-out night dreams rather than plausible daydreams.

The first step in recovering your dreams is to memorize and repeat the SQUARE TWO MANTRA: *There are no rules, and that's okay.*

This doesn't mean that you take all constraints off your behavior; it means that you begin operating out of the curiosity and passion of your essential self, rather than the fear and propriety of your social self.

Forming a goal, especially if you write it down and visualize it, creates a search image that programs your brain to focus on anything resembling or leading to that objective.

As your plan becomes more thorough, your research more complete, and the steps to your goal easier to envision, you'll find yourself developing a kind of impatience to actually go out and *do it*.

SQUARE THREE:
THE HERO'S SAGA

*The journey of a
thousand miles begins from
beneath your feet.*

—LAO-TZU

IF YOUR GOAL is true and heartfelt, the journey through Square Three is guaranteed to be terrifying, exhausting, and incredibly exhilarating.

All dreams are realized through pragmatic action. Magic really does follow longing and intention, but it usually ends up looking quite ordinary.

ACCELERATING FROM ZERO

1) Break every task into turtle steps. A "turtle step" is is my label for the largest possible task that your essential self can do easily.

2) Bribe your essential self.

3) Do a terrible job.
With time and practice, you'll do
your North Star tasks brilliantly.
But being willing to make a mess is
a prerequisite to gaining that skill.

FAILURE

A WILLINGNESS to make mistakes and
recover from them is absolutely
essential gear for getting you through
the rocky, treacherous territory you'll
hit. .... Square Three is the region of
trial and error, not perfection.

1) Hang loose. Try to relax, observe, and relinquish your expectation.

2) Learn from your mistakes.

3) Go back to Square One. The way to analyze a failed Square Three effort is to let it knock you back—or, rather, on—to Square One. A major failure should be a "catalytic event" that jolts you into letting go of your agenda. ... Was your failure a result of inadequately defining your dreams?

4) Repeat the SQUARE THREE MANTRA. It goes:

This is much worse than I expected, and that's okay.

5) If you can't figure out what's wrong, just do something different.

In his book *Do One Thing Different*, psychotherapist Bill O'Hanlon recommends that if you can't figure out what you're doing to create a pattern of failure, you should just change something—anything.

SUCCESS

A HERO'S SAGA doesn't end with a single triumph; the sooner the hero slays his first enemy, the sooner he gets to meet the dragon, and the Orcs, and the evil sorcerer. It's just one damn thing after another. So after taking time to savor the sweet taste of victory, get set to do the following:

1) Work like a dog.

When you're headed for your own North Star, you'll find yourself doing the work you were meant for, the work that was meant for you. You, too, will bounce out of bed clamoring to get on with it. You'll work long hours without even noticing they've gone by.

2) Play like a dog.

The more intensely you have to work, the more you need to take play breaks. Playing improves your creativity and problem-solving skills, minimizes burnout, and maintains high-level performance.

3) Hang out with your favorite people.

You'll find your own North Star peopled not with folks you merely like but those you genuinely adore. These people will share your passions and ideals. Their essential selves are likely to fit beautifully with yours. They are your tribe.

SQUARE FOUR:
THE PROMISED LAND

On the path to excellence, the gods have placed many obstacles, and the way is steep and hard to climb. But when you get to the top, then it is easy, even though it is hard.

—HESIOD

You'll know you've arrived in Square Four when your dreams have not only come true but demonstrated some long-term staying power.

Once you've reached Square Four and things are going your way, for heaven's sake, ease up. In Square Four, less effort equals more security and accomplishment.

Don't throw your precious time and energy into low-yield strategies. If something drains you dry while contributing very little to your success, don't do it.

Focus on becoming really, really good at the things that will sustain your success.

A hoarding mentality actually keeps you from experiencing joy, reduces your ability to make money, and scuttles both personal and professional relationships.

Stinginess isn't just unattractive; it's counterproductive.

People who express gratitude create pools of generosity in the world around them.

BE HERE NOW

There is beauty before me, and
there is beauty behind me.
There is beauty to my left, and
there is beauty to my right.
There is beauty above me, and
there is beauty below me.
There is beauty around me, and
there is beauty within me.

—"THE BEAUTY WAY"
Navajo prayer-chant

Repeat the Beauty Way chant right now, wherever you are. You'll begin to notice beauty, all kinds of beauty, everywhere—in birdsongs and battle cries, muscles and equations, angst and oatmeal. You will discover what it is to be present.

So you've finally slowed down and begun to enjoy the abundant life of the promised land.

You cannot control anyone else's journey through life. Focus on your own. Compassion, honesty, self-scrutiny, and an open mind are the only "one way" to interact sanely and successfully with others.

The life you put together in the outside world must accommodate the reality of change.... Learn to follow the flow, do-without-doing, fully experience surprise, tragedy, delight, and wonder as they come your way. In practical terms, this means not overburdening yourself with so much doing that you have no time to be.

Repeat the
Square Four Mantra:

Everything is changing,
and that's okay.

AND FINALLY...

ALL OF THE ADVICE in this book
boils down to just one thing: You are
designed with the ability to find the
life you were meant to live. No one
but you has the ability to find your
own North Star, and no one but you
has the power to keep you from finding it. No one.

Your own North Star is not a
place but a state of being. You are the
best destination you could possibly
imagine or experience.

Welcome home.